As If the World
Made Sense

New Poems by Maude Meehan

OTHER BOOKS BY MAUDE MEEHAN
Chipping Bone
Before the Snow
Washing the Stones

As If the World Made Sense

Maude Meehan

Many Names Press
Capitola, California

ISBN: 0-9652575-9-2
Library of Congress Control Number: 2003109946

Cover art, "Question of Balance" © 2003 James Aschbacher
Maude Meehan photo © Dottie Jakobsen

Jacket and book design © 2003 Kate Hitt
katehitt@manynamespress.com

Grateful acknowledgement is made to the following publications
which first published some of the material in this book:
Caesura; Quarry West: Celebration of the Muse anthology;
*Sarasota Review of Poetry; June Cotner's Blessings, Weddings,
Mothers and Daughters, and Family* anthologies; *Women in
Libraries; Presentation Hall; Silent Voices; Metro Active Books;
The Blue Moon Review;* The Santa Cruz *Sentinel; Illusion of
Light; Somebody's Speaking My Language; Proposing on the
Brooklyn Bridge; Poets for Peace; Toward That Sacred Stone*

Lillian Heritage, Editor

Jacket printing by Community Printers, Santa Cruz, California

Interior manufacturing by Malloy on acid-free recycled paper
containing a minimum of 85% recovered fiber
with 30% post consumer waste

⊛

For Lucille Clifton
sister woman
with great love
for her light
her vision
her amazing poetry
her incredible being
her great heart

ACKNOWLEDGMENTS

To my children, Donna, Chris, Charles and their families for
their ever present love, support and enrichment of my life.

To Lillian Heritage, beloved friend and invaluable editor,
without whose steadfast commitment, diligence, patience
and constant encouragement this book would still be
only random scraps of paper, my everlasting gratitude.

To my dear Kate Luna, whose loving spirit, wisdom
and presence have been a constant in my life,
my heartfelt thanks for urging that I make my work
a priority, thereby midwifing this book.

For years of warmest friendship, support and inspiration,
my writing group—Kathryn Chetkovich, Frances Hatfield,
Lillian Heritage, Joan McMillan, Amber Coverdale Sumrall,
Dena Taylor & Ellen Treen.

Special appreciation to Ellen Bass, Barbara Brautigam,
Jerry Burke, Lucille Clifton, Steven Gulie, Kate Hitt,
Rick Hochler, Jim and Jeanne Wakatsuki Houston,
Akasha Hull, Stephen Kessler, Morton Marcus,
Julie Olsen Edwards, Celine Marie Pascale, Linda Selby,
Claire Braz Valentine, Patrice Vecchione, & Gary Young,
for long years of faith and friendship.

CONTENTS

How It Was

Evolution

What Endures

Going Through Arsenic

Yerba Maté

Whistle Stop

HOW IT WAS

Poems for Acer

*We have connections with one another
that are more important than life or death.*

—Issan, Buddhist priest

PART I

....in precious moments
I have felt what it means to be wild and free.

—Susanna Moodie

HOW IT WAS
Zoar Valley 1970

Back country road
steamy
summer night
saddled behind you
arms
circling your waist
legs
straddling
your thighs
face
burrowed
between
shoulder blades
breasts pressed
against
strong
solid shelter
of your back
sultry wind
rushing past
carrying
your scent

hot shaft
of headlight
piercing
pitch dark
heated
roar
of engine
pulsing
wanting

to ride
forever

Intensive Care
1959

You sat uneasy
Looked away
from this wan stranger
from dangling I.V. tubes
stained dressings
and searched for conversation
Mentioned in passing
that our youngest
said he could not remember
how I looked. Added
that since I'd been away
he hadn't made his lion
roar noise in the morning
when he woke. Then your voice
broke, and I, flooded with longing
helpless with anger at my body's
treachery, began to weep
The nurse dismissed you, saying
"What she needs is sleep."

4

RARE GIFT
1990

This man, not given to bringing flowers
unexpected gifts, or easy compliments
once asked if there was anything I wished
I could have been or done,
or had missed out on, in our long years together.

Yes, I answered, but don't laugh
I've always wished I could write music
the kind of songs that people would remember
Smiling, he shook his head and said
"But your whole life has been a song."

I wrapped his words in sudden warmth
and put them carefully away
against the day when I might need their comfort.

Remembered Gift
1991

The curl
       of tongue
              on tongue
smooth length
         of thigh
              on thigh
soft moan
        outcry
           wild spinning
                 high
          slow
      spiral
down
        this flowing
            overflowing
                gift
to one another

Part II

What does it mean, to sing of grief over and over,
to immerse in the mysteries of fluid and bone
until the heart is washed cleaner than wood
left open to the rain's touch and the sun's slow fingers....

—Joan McMillan
June Elegy

STORM RESIDUE

1991

Last night torrential rains
licked with a frenzied
tongue at loosened shingles
mottled the ceilings
with dark spittle.

Unruly winds
sent branches crashing
to the ground
outside the window
where I lay huddled, sleepless.

This morning thunder rumbles
then recedes beyond the mountains
where early light reveals
trestles that sag askew
and shattered stumps
in still damp air that bears
the oily scent of eucalyptus.

I make my way
down the steep
mud-slippery path,
anxious to see how the small harbor
and its craft have fared.

The decks of sailing boats
that daily braceleted
the long curved arm of the horizon
are littered with everything
not battened down,
but rocking gently, safely tethered.

Sand weighted waves
still spill storm residue
along the ravaged shore
where back and forth a seal
humps restlessly, relentlessly
across debris strewn sand
barking its plaintive cry
back arched, head craned
and searching vainly out to sea.

I feel a sudden surge of empathy
flow toward this creature,
who seems like me,
distraught and raw with longing
in my life's aftermath of havoc.

LIAR, LIAR, PANTS ON FIRE
1992

You said my coccyx fractured not because I fell skiing
but because I spent a lifetime sitting on the fence
looking at both sides of the question.

When we were kids you said a whole lot of stuff.
Mostly you said you'd always, always
stay beside me, never leave
not for anything, not for anyone.

You told a whole bunch of lies
but I didn't care because
you were everything I ever wanted
and you were a whole lot of fun
and you kissed so good

I don't laugh as much these days.
Now my mouth just hurts most the time
it needs kissing so bad

Would you believe,

I even dreamed that Dennis Rodman, yes, I said
Dennis Rodman, drove up in a big red truck
and took me for a nice long ride and gave me
a nice long kiss.

Well I always did like bad boys
and I guess he's about the baddest.
Anyway it's your fault I kissed Dennis Rodman back.

Just pence on that awhile.

And when everybody talks you up I get a bad case of
charisma bypass and want to say things like
"Yeah, well he always left the seat up,"
and like what a big liar you were 'cause you left me
and you promised you wouldn't, not ever.

But looking at both sides of the question,
it wasn't your fault, you couldn't help it;
just the same I get mad sometimes;
you shouldn't have died first, you promised.

MAY RETROGRADE
1993

Eggshell nights
tear open

no light enters

again

I watch death
wrap you
in her shroud

leaving for me
this shawl of snakes
I cannot shed

It holds no warmth

no promise
no relief

HEAT WAVE
August, 1994

Too much, this heavy scent
of jasmine that fevers
the night air

Lemons hang full and ready
exploding as they fall to ground
spraying a sharp-sweet mist

All is so lush, so overripe
that I implode, taut with desire
alone, in this cold winter of my life

EPILOGUE
Summer 1996

What amazes
is that so much
remains the same.
Your keys hang
in the usual place,
cars stitch the road
and planes drone overhead.

In the market
where I go daily
to escape the silence
business goes on
as if the world made sense.

I choose this head of
lettuce over that,
these plums,
as if it mattered.
Tinned music
fills the aisles,
mangles a ballad
we once loved.

Now I sit in this pub
to pass the time
waiting for food
I do not want,
to stave off — not hunger — but
return to emptiness.

And no one here
or anywhere I turn
can tell me how
or why, or even if
it will be possible
to survive
engulfed
in wanting you,
wanting you back,
alive.

Three A.M. Snow Drift

1937   You walked me home through the lamplit park
and unexpected snow. Soft flakes, so thick,
so round, the kind that cling and glitter
under light, familiar landscape changing
into mysterious terrain. In that
hushed world you turned and kissed me,
flakes melting on my upturned face,
the night a dazzle of promise

1947   We drove for hours through the storm,
soft whispery hum of the old heater,
a rhythmic swish of wipers, were
the only sounds. Bright crystals
swirled, danced in the headlights
on the winding country roads.
Content, I rested close
in the haven of your warmth,
the baby sleeping in my arms
and safely reaching home you leaned
to take our child, and kissed me

1967   When our children were grown,
gone off to their own lives,
we often skied cross-country through
the neighbors' land. Their old pony
fat in his shaggy winter coat, ghostlike
in falling snow, snorted a cloud of greeting
as we crossed his path. Later,
stopping across the field, you bent
in the hushed dark, kissed me, and with
the sting of frozen flakes against my skin
spun the years sweetly, swiftly backward

1997   Now I wake restless in this warm
west coast town long miles and years away
from winter snow, and rise to make
this cage of words to hold recaptured memories

LADY FINGERS

2000

You used to like to tell about when you were six
and traveling with your mother
to visit cousins in Virginia.
How you came down with typhoid
and were delirious and deathly sick
for days in a hotel in Washington D. C.
How you woke up at last,
and nothing would satisfy your hunger
but Lady Fingers from Novotny's.

But Novotny's was back in New York City,
on 86th and 6th, and it was weeks
before you stood before that altar
foregoing eclairs, Napoleons, sprinkled cupcakes
for those delicate, powdered-sugar-dusted
Lady Finger treats. I used to buy them for you,
but first Novotny's, then Lady Fingers, disappeared.

For years you spoke as if it were
a personal affront that bakeries
no longer seemed to make or even know
about them anymore; it must be
thirty, forty years since I last saw one.

Today walking through Trader Joe's
to my delight up there right on the shelf

were Lady Fingers, large as life.
Though you've been dead these five long years,
I thought, "Oh wait till Ace sees these,"
then stood transfixed, as if you too
had shown up, suddenly risen from the past.

And I fled blindly, leaving my cart in the damn aisle,
wanting to call out,
"Hey Honey I found Lady Fingers,"
tears coursing unexpected, as the sharp stab
of lady hunger that welled up in me.

Tomorrow I'll go back and buy some just to show
your grandsons, tell them the way you used to
tell me of that trip you took when you were
just about their age, as if it had a special magic.

How your hillbilly cousins greeted your cityfolk arrival
with banjos, fiddle music and ripe watermelon
and how you watched in awe as toothless old
Grand-Aunt Sary, lips flapping, spat the seeds
past the porch railing, aiming and cackling
when she zapped the sleeping hounds. I'll tell them
as I pass the soft sweet Lady Fingers round
and know somehow I'm passing on a share of you.

EPIPHANIES
2002

Such change aloneness makes
in one's perceptions;
Each would have sworn
we gave the other room to grow
to know ourselves as individuals
and more than most we did.

Now looking inward is a constant
and a sharp clarity emerges
sometimes comforting
though just as often painful.
I long to share with you
these insights that lay dormant
through the years that you were here.

Epiphanies like arrows
lit with sunlight
or with flame pierce holes
in old assumptions,
all the blind double bind
of being half an entity.
I see us now, not as reflected

in one another's' gaze
glazed over time with expectations
habit or desire, but as we were
flawed, foolish and content.

I think back on those easy
mornings, the way we sat
disheveled bookends
propped in our bed
sharing black coffee
small talk, the paper,
drifting so carelessly
so blindly into each day.

Now I am routed out of bed
by nearby empty space
as tangible as touch,
waking to find myself
a sudden stranger
with two shadows

MARKERS
2002

Today I wandered through shady stillness
of the old cemetery reading epitaphs on
family stones.
A common pastime of the bereaved.
Sitting on the bench beneath your tree
I told you of the Asian girl named Kim
whose favorite dog was pictured,
carved next to lines relating simply that
she was seventeen and had been murdered.

A woman whose gravestone reads
"Yard Sales Forever" close by a boy
whose name was Miguelito.
The small white picket fence around his grave
a silent playpen, strewn with worn toys.

I felt you listening as I described the one
you would be drawn to,
scattered with beer cans,
full and empty, notes now illegible,
some plastic flowers, biker gear,
a rough wooden slab hand printed "Lil Richard
My Hero, A Man Whose Father Is Proud"

How austere the gravestone that you wanted.
Just name, your date of birth and death,

no honors listed, no naval title,
no board of surgeons' blather.
If there was anything that you rejected
it was what you called braggadocio,
though later I felt compelled to add a marker,
bronze, small and plain, your nickname "ACE"
engraved, making you somehow
more accessible, certain you wouldn't mind.

I know that there are only ashes here
but find some comfort in this ritual
which brings you near. Just as when
your voice begins to fade from memory
it feels as if I'm losing you again,
I take the tape of your last call
from where I keep it safe,
press the remote and once again
your presence fills dead space.

EVOLUTION

Flowering must come from the roots.

—Greg Keith
Life Near 310° Kelvin

JAMES
Chichester, England 1843-1926

Arrogant self-styled aristocrat
whom no one dared call Jim, reed thin
and elegant, divinely proper
as a gift from God of course would be,
claimed kinship with Elizabeth, the poet,
his surname being Barrett.
He had a certain cool cachet
laced with an icy caustic wit,
his usual lemon twist of irony
felt, if not understood
by us, his grandchildren,
whom he would fix with
baleful poached-egg eyes,
interrogate, then with sharp rap
of silver-headed cane dismiss us,
returning to his Havanese cigar
and evening paper, or leaning back
assume a lofty, far away expression
while at his behest, my mother,
youngest daughter, played Chopin etudes,
or Bach's elegant abstractions.

His word was law to those who came
within its jurisdiction, and to Liz, his wife
who bore him sixteen children.
She was fourteen when they were wed.
Not so unusual in an era when, if you lived past
childhood, survival of the fittest was the test
and most were laid to rest by forty-five. James bested
all statistics, having survived till eighty-four,
but as seemed only fitting, Liz outlived him.

LIZ
Kent, England 1846-1928

It was rumoured
James had played fast and loose
with family funds, and so
was banished to America.
All we know for certain is
that Liz sailed aboard a schooner
with three small children, pregnant again,
and carrying a tasseled satin reticule
embroidered by her sister,
heavy with hoarded sovereigns
and bits of jewelry
pressed on her by her mother
for the journey home, should the new world
and life with errant James prove more misfortune.
The purse was stolen from her storm-tossed cabin
as she lay watching, helpless, sick to death.

At forty-five, when Liz was close to term
carrying my mother, who would be
the last of twelve surviving children,
her eldest son was struck down
by a chance runaway horse and carriage.
Later, when going through his bureau, Liz found

an envelope containing savings, earmarked, *For Ma,*
to travel home and see her family. But she never did.

Liz kept a sweetness, an almost childlike innocence,
that even I, a young girl when she died,
could recognize, and oh, I would have watched
forever when she brushed her white and waist length
hair before the angled mirror of her dressing table,
where she let me play, tracing
the curly letters of her monogram on silver bowls,
or winding combings for the flowerlets she made.
I still, at seventy-five can sew almost invisible
fine seams or darn frayed cloth,
weaving the thread the way she
taught me and my elder sister so patiently. Lately
she visits, cossets me, as she did years and years ago.
With her is my mother, and I awaken, smiling.

INHERITANCE
Edgar Maxwell Gruen, 1884-1973

Against a painted backdrop a child
stares warily into the camera. He is
three, wears high button shoes,
black stockings, and a knee length
tartan, his sad, imperious face
framed by ringlets and lace collar.

It is my father. The photo yields small clue
to the brooding parent whom I knew as
paradox. Prone to deep melancholy, he saw
shades of darkness everywhere although
his moods were well disguised in public

He died, bequeathing to me that stealthy
phantom cat of ever-present angst
to claw at me, to come and go at will
twitching its tail, grooming its ragged
fur, mewling a thin deceitful purr.

INDOCTRINATION

for my mother and grandmother

These women
imparted knowledge
drawn from
deep reservoirs
of strength
Tended
the weak and sick
eased painful movement
in and out of life
Instilled in daughters, sisters
who would take their place
the grace of calm compassion

APOLOGIA

for my daughter, 1990

If in my fear for you
I tied your spirit
when it longed to fly
or if messages I gave
in early years were
mixed, and now seem
lies that fed on fantasies
of bridal veils and cribs
and ever, ever after,
believe me that I tried
the only way I knew
to shield you in a world
that did not then or now
safeguard its women,
and had I warned you
would you have believed?

Like my compliant mother
we all for generations back
were raised on dreams
and fears, and only in late
years have learned that we
must heal ourselves.

Sometimes through lonely
painful flight, sometimes
through struggling to fight
to stand on still uncertain ground.

I watch with pride
as you break free, learning
far more of honesty
than you once learned from me.

SOLACE

Alone now
and too wakeful
I listen
to taped words
of other poets
only to find
it is my own
verse
that soothes me
then recognize
familiar cadence
my mother's voice
in mine
lulling me softly
safely
into sleep

Message In May
for baby Mark, 1956

Frozen in my own grief
I found it somehow strangely right
that snow fell yesterday

Not that thick winter snow
that blankets the bleakest landscape
with its short-lived purity
but a sparse sleety fall, only enough
to mute the acrid green of astro-turf
laid to conceal that dark pit, freshly spaded

I placed tight buds of yellow roses
in beside you, later more
across your small white
almost weightless coffin, then
watched it lowered down beyond my reach

This morning remnants of snow
still lay in patches on our lawn, yet
in the cold dark of that cruel night
a cut-back, wild and never blooming bush
unfurled small perfect yellow roses to the
morning light.

MARRIAGE BLESSING
for our children

Your parents, we who love you
and all our children more than life itself,
have looked on in joy, recognizing
that in your desire to create a future together
you have discovered and have fostered
one another's most endearing and enduring qualities.

The love we have for you is all embracing,
joyful, to see you turn toward one another's light.
Certain that you will tenderly support each other,
aware that patience as much as passion
will nourish and maintain the bond between you.
Certain also, that with care and courage you will
create a haven where each may grow and flourish
as do all things in nature given light and warmth.

We who watched over your childhood innocence
with the most profound longing
to keep you from all hurt or harm,
no longer yearn toward that gift
which is not ours to give,
for we have learned that adversity
brings its own gifts of strength and of compassion.

As you set out upon the path
which we have traveled, we stand beside you
with every confidence in your resilience and strength.
As we once cradled you in strong young arms
we hold you now, as strongly, sweetly, in our hearts.
How very proud of you we are. Know that you have
our blessing, as you know you have our love.

EVOLUTION

Six month old
grandson Sam
all flailing limbs
and sputtery face
laughs with delight
as tightly held
he thrashes
in deep water

Oh brave small
pollywog
how comforting
to feel such trust
as with each thrust
you harken back
to your beginnings

Nonsense Song for a Grandbaby

Squishable
squashable
sweetable lamb
scrunchable
squeezable
plump little man
soon you'll be crawling
and trying to stand

Milky sweet
silky skinned
silly small Sam
please stay a baby
as long as you can

GRANDSONS

Yesterday Reilly
just getting over being sick
ate only half his pizza slice
and said, no thanks
he didn't want an ice cream cone.
You understand, this is a first
considering it is his chosen
favorite 'lunch with grandma' menu.

He waited patiently
as older brother Sam
ordered a two scoop sundae
a kid ice cream concoction
called, it's true, believe it
Dirt and Worms.

As Reilly watched Sam ferret out
and chew each gummi worm
spooning the melting cream
and sticky chocolate syrup, his face was soft
suffused with rapt, vicarious pleasure

and then, when Sam in sympathy
proffered the last spoonful
complete with worm
and dripping gunky sauce
he took it, head tilted back,
mouth opened wide as any
fledgling. Then said *thank you*
with the grateful fervor, reserved
—at least in my experience—
for saviors and true heroes.

They walked back to the car
as close as twins joined at the hip
climbed in, leaned shoulder to shoulder
each in his own way sweetly surfeited.

OBSERVING SLATER
grandson

I. AT TWO

Intrepid acrobat
adventurer
you run and climb
exploring everything

Each new day's offerings
eagerly embraced
in a bright world where
everything it seems
exists for your delight

Night holds no terrors
in your safe domain
and fear is not a word
you comprehend

Beguiling boy
maelstrom of energy
it's rare to see
such confidence
such derring-do
in one whose years
add only up to two

OBSERVING SLATER

II. AT SIX

Each day holds mystery
and surprise when you
young sponge
awaken, eager to absorb

Team player
budding jock
your room's awash
in uniforms, headgear
skates, bats and balls
of every known variety

Still you devour every kind
of book you find
the way that many hunger
after candy, and most
amazing, you think school is fun

You choose to study violin
prefer the opera *Carmen*
sung in language you don't
understand, to children's
fare like *Annie, Peter Pan*

Beguiling boy, your
mama's joy, your papa's star
how I wonder what you are
what will you do, who will you be?

I wish that I could live to see.   43

Boy Song

for my great grandson Ryder

I press the rewind cue, you vanish
into the box that brought your image
thousands of miles from the East Coast
to play inside the quiet of my room.

These seven years past you've morphed
on film, infant to warrior in kid karate garb
or on a bicycle streak across the screen,
young Mercury, in winged sneaks and helmet.

This time I see you sit, composed, straight
backed, trying to tell me of your school
while baby sister pokes her head
into the camera's eye and chatters
at this old person whom she does not know.

How patiently you wait. And I, impatient,
long to reach into the screen and bring you
to my side, to know once more your scent,
trace with my hands familiar features
that bear your father's stamp.

When he was just about your age he came
to visit us, and when asked what was the most
important thing in life, pondered a moment,
then, dead serious, responded, "Breath."

44

And how I hope you will breathe deeply,
of love and laughter, even tragedy and pain,
inhaling *all* with hungry passion, so when you
are old like me, the answer still will be the same.

In a few months a new tape will arrive.
You will be older, taller, moving further into
boyhood. But for now, I see and hear you
in my heart, a far off song. It bears your name.

SAVANNAH TERESE
great granddaughter

Miles distant
a newborn
who has as yet
no secrets lies
no existential angst
nor even laughter
enters this life
luminous and clear
as hope in darkness

Small slate
on whom the world
already writes
its coded messages
in undetermined script
may you be wise
as you are welcome
blessed always
and surrounded
as you are now
by love

Symbiosis

When he was small
and slumbering
our youngest son
rocked nightly
in his crib
thumping the wall
the floor
thudding from side to side
like some hypnotic metronome

In an adjacent bed
his brother
deep in sleep
his breathing
neatly timed
lay motionless
except for one small foot
dancing a sprightly counterpoint

AT EIGHTY

This morning, I tuned out the news,
unplugged the phone
opened the back door
inhaled delicious fresh
spring air, and wondered
who could ask for more

I couldn't help delighting
in the pecky sound of birds
out on the deck
plucking at mounds of lint
I'd saved all year from my old dryer

I always set them out
on the first sunny day
imagining nestlings,
cozy in fluff from
fuzzies saved all year

Why, only yesterday I had fun finding
Easter cards and baskets
for my grand and great grandchildren,

oh, and I treated myself to a CD by
Santana, that sent blood coursing
madly through my varicosities.
And furthermore, last night I had a dream
no nice old white-haired, widdy woman
is supposed to have, what's more
I thoroughly enjoyed it

So though my wild and woolly days are past
don't for a moment think
that you have heard the last
from this old lady, and did I
mention by the way that when
I heal and throw away this cane
I have on layaway a big red Harley?

NOTES FROM A GERIATRIC DIVA
At 83

Sunday afternoon, radio playing rainy day music.
It's been pouring for days. I've been going through
old photos of friends, relatives, past gatherings
teasing a kaleidoscope of joyful and melancholy recollections.

This one, a song-filled celebration with new friends
taken more than thirty years ago, when we moved from
the east coast to Santa Cruz. We found ourselves among
a varied mix of long-haired poets, artists, surfers who
welcomed us by helping to unload our belongings.

We were starting a new life from scratch among
the gentlest people we have known. To one side
of our cottage lived earth mother Apple, and Spirit,
a sandal-maker PhD, with their dog Cannabis and a cat
called Silly whose whole name was Psilocybin.

They brought into our lives a host of friends,
some of whom have moved away since Santa Cruz
became a pricey place to stay. And I won't forget those
three dear gay men friends, lost that first epidemic year
to AIDS. First Little John, and Larry, then Daniel,
gifted concert pianist, the last to go.
I still miss them, miss their wit and loyal friendship,
still have red ribbons in a drawer.

Now and then I run into some of the old crowd, now
upright ordinary citizens. No longer driving beat up vans,
but SUVs, working in real estate, or silicon valley.
Tie dye and patches abandoned, along with dreams
of a caring, kinder world.

Oh, here's a photo, wide angle, of my younger brother's
wedding reception, more than forty friends and family
captured clapping and smiling as the cake is cut.
Now only five of us remain – myself, my older brother,
two cousins and the bride, now nearing eighty and
long since a widow.

Days spin to weeks, and months, then years, like
pinwheels in high wind, and so much still to do.
I make small foolish bargains with capricious Fate.
Barter for time to finish this or that, knowing full
well how she springs swift surprises.

At any rate I see time's at its usual tricks,
and I must tidy up this heap, reminders of a
rich plum pudding past, and ease back into my
daily world, a strange well-meant arrangement
called *assisted living*. I've already missed this
afternoon's *Activities*: Armchair Aerobics, Nickel Bingo
and good old Benjy on the Banjo. Well, if I hurry
I can make it down in time for Cut-Throat Dominoes
and dinner.

REMEMBERING CHRISTMAS, 1925

Morning at last. The tree, decked in shining ornaments
as we slept. The cup of milk empty, just crumbs
from cookies on Santa's plate. Pungent odor of pine,
candle wax. Sound of thick bright papers tearing, crisp
crumple of tissue. Cries of surprise, pleasure.
Ribbons everywhere.

Special pastries for breakfast, and Mama busy
in the kitchen. Late morning, Uncle Maximilian's
chauffeur delivers the annual basket... Uncle Max and
Aunt Cora wait in the car outside. Daddy says they're
busy and have to make a lot of stops, like Santa.
My big brother said Aunt Cora is sickly. She has
a creaky, crabby voice. He said she's rich as Croesus.
I don't know who that was.

The basket is piled high with chocolate from Perugia,
jams, jellies, lemon curd, beaded cookies, crackers,
strange smelling cheeses, and best of all,
almond scented Marzipan shaped into tiny fruits
and flowers. Treats foreign as Father's favourite
basket gifts, the long graceful bottles, their contents
amber, topaz, ruby — as father holds them
to the light, he reads each beautiful label aloud:
Madeira, Muscatel, Chablis, Claret, Tokay.
I taste the names, the colors, the sound of his
pleasure, round as sugar pebbles rolling on my tongue.

On the mantel, the crèche, manger strewn
with shredded wheat for straw. The Holy Family,
shepherds, donkeys, and camels. The Three Kings
with gifts of incense and myrrh for baby Jesus.
Incense always makes me cough in church.
Myrrh has the sound of kitty purring.

The doorbell rings again and again. Aunts, uncles,
grandparents, and best of all, the cousins arrive.
We play games, laugh too loud, run too fast. Banished
to the big bedroom, still giggling.

Leaves stretch the dining room table. Tall candles
flicker. Mr. Turkey wears fat sprigs of parsley.
Great mounds of mashed potatoes, brimming gravy boats,
Mama's special bread dressing, spicy with
Bells poultry seasoning. All manner of vegetables
that I don't have to eat this day.

And oh, at last, the plum pudding, wreathed
with holly and dancing flames of brandy.
A crystal bowl of hard sauce, smooth and creamy
despite its name; decorated by me and my big sister with
tiny leaves from the hedge and bright red maraschino
cherries we cut to look like poinsettias.

The great big round gold ornament Grandma Henrietta
brought with her from Denmark hangs on green satin
ribbon from the chandelier. We children take turns
standing beneath it, necks arched to capture
our reflection.

Mouths stretched in huge-toothed grins, convex eyes,
and disappearing chins. Grotesque as gargoyles,
our faces distorted yet eerily familiar doppelgangers.
It makes me wonder, a beautiful globe
with power to make us ugly.

Later, my mother's hands bring beauty from the old
upright piano. Her sweet soprano, my father's
rich baritone, harmonizing old favorites, *Just a Song at
Twilight, Macushla, I'll Take You Home Again Kathleen.*
Goose-bump shivers when Daddy sings *Sea Fever.*
My pride wanting to burst.

Then night time, grownup time. Rise and fall
of laughter, known voices spill from the living room.
My bedroom door opened a small crack,
not wanting to let go the day.

Conjuring the tree, the painted birds with feather tails
clipped to top branches, the gleaming ornaments,
silver icicles, and underneath heaped gifts for all.

My stocking surprises, a bracelet of tiny garnets,
fuzzy mittens, a puzzle ball, a little clown dolly, nuts,
hard candies, and the best treat lumping the toe,
a tangerine in winter.

Under the tree my first real ice skates, no more double
runners. Holding my breath, opening a big doll trunk
that held matching flowered dresses my Grandma Liz
made for next summer. One for me and one for
my dolly Emma, and a pale pink parasol for each.
Mine has ruffles. This is the best Christmas.

My little brother asleep in his crib. He got lots and lots
of toys but only wanted his squishy old monkey.
When I was little as him I took all my presents to bed
with me. I hear the sound of carolers outside, and
I want to get up and peek, but am sleepy warm under
my soft quilt. Faces, voices and pictures rush by as if
I'm riding a merry-go-round, whirling faster, faster,
whirling, whirling....

WHAT ENDURES

*The writer is a witness who struggles not
to flinch, not to look away.*

—Sam Hamill

*I will not pretend to see less than I do
to make them comfortable.*

—Irene McKinney

WHAT ENDURES

The child is naked
takes her seat at the table

eyes turn
staccato chatter ceases
a finger of expectation
laid across lips

Dead Alice
hands her a fan
Her first grade teacher
his handkerchief

From small numb fingers
they drop to the floor

The children   all but herself
are sent from the table
Father Xavier makes
the sign of the cross
follows them quickly

Sister Penitentia skitters after
on stiletto heels   Stains of red
lace and satin
flash beneath vestments

The diners clap, laughing

Head turned away
her mother weeps black tears

Only her brother   his eyes
dark as their fathers longing
covers her
with childhood's quilt

Sleep seeps slowly
from the woman

What lingers
odor of candles   incense
shame

MUMMY
1976

she has covered
herself
arrayed herself in

         yes

leans into mirrors
into eyes
reflecting

         yes

each day winds
layer on layer
binds

         yes

around her life

MOUSE DREAMS

Do you see how they come
these nibbling grey dreams,
how I wake to faint echoes
shards of shadow and light
escaping just as their shapes
tease recognition? Do you know
how I stalk them, cat on a leash?

Do you see how they torment,
spiteful as alpha siblings
demanding a turn, taking mine
flashing glimpses of razors,
guns, palm size, *easy to hide.*
How they offer their pretty pills,
dangle release, promising peace?

Do you see how they proffer a carving knife,
prod and poke at this no-more-wife?
I'll cut off their tails with my children's life.
See how I run, see how I run, run, run?

GONE

for Greg Keith
10/11/45–6/8/98

Outside along the deck Tibetan prayer flags
stir. All else is still.
Indoors the old guitar rests in its case
reminder of the long while since you pleasured us
with sweet, or sad, or bawdy ballads.

Here in your home we women gather
in age old ritual, the scent and sound of you
still palpable in air. The myriad books
that could not sate your hungry mind
are everywhere, stacked on tall shelves,
piled on the table where you worked,
its surface still awash in papers, poems
that often spilled unnoticed to the floor.

Late in the morning, clumsy despite all care
we bump and back and turn through narrow doors
bearing your wasted body.

Time now to wrap your lanky, long-boned self
in chosen cloth, close the hard cover
bright with flowers, poems and pictures,
and in a last gesture of respect and love
we women *"heft"* as you would have said,
the heavy weight, carry your coffin down
worn, wooden, vine-wrapped stairs, to where
black-suited strangers wait to drive you off.

We linger on the lawn, bereft,
uncertain what to do after long months of vigil.
Then, turn and return as women always have
to what you called *"life's dailies."* Dull tasks
still necessary to perform, that neither fill
the void nor ease the pain, yet being so mundane
are sharp reminders of lost brilliance from our lives.

EMERGENCY
response to K.N.

So having slit my soul
dark blood invisible

wrists neatly in my lap
attached

to hands
pretending innocence

I read the ashes
of the book you burned

language familiar
reasons
      excuses
          mine:

my animal self crawls back
to that black place

waits
      for fire
          light
            to die
nothing
      everything

is an emergency

riddle

what is
heavy as his left hand
silent as his right
creeps into your little room
in the stilly night
what is the answer
don't tell it if you know
your little lips will blister
your body turn to snow

HER CHOICE
my own Auntie Mame

She called to say goodbye
said she was going home
She called, wanted to say thank you
for what I can't remember

My idol when I was a child
she danced her way past disapproving aunties
into a world where women were called flappers,
adventurous ones who dared
to show bare knees, to wear bobbed hair,
and in her beaded bag, a long, slim holder, gold,
for cigarettes, Gauloise from Paris
a silver flask for gin

At eighty she owned a chequered
past of roller-coastered years
furs and diamonds, an illustrious career
Bittersweet memories of a handsome
ne'er do well, then later
a steady man, ambitious as herself

She called to say goodbye, said thank you
said, you know I've always loved you
I answered be safe, you know I love you too
Call me when you come back

Later that day, all phone calls made
the mandatory notes inscribed, the time
arrived for sweet relief of hoarded capsules
downed with a crystal glass of finest Scotch
She left with the same panache
as she had lived her eighty years

There were those who called it selfish;
as for me those last few years
I could scarcely bear to see
her spirit fade, dwindle
like her waning world.
Goodbye old girl, and I say Bravo

An Imminence of Wings

The grove of eucalyptus has been slashed
great wings of wild Blue Herons no longer
cleave the air   tall stately cranes
have disappeared along with
raucous starlings and the chirp of
small brave sparrows from branches
where they had welcomed sunrise

A silence palpable as pain
now underscores the loss
of so much and so many dearly loved
these past long weightful years

Only the shadow bird I dread returns.
I listen, alert for a remembered sound
its sharp beak at the fragile pane
fearing that I will hear again
the sound of shattering glass

Déjà Vue Winter, 2003

Shots ring out in classrooms
Suffer the little children
Guns in their hands

Vets hunker in doorways
Embalmed by their past
Blood in their dreams

Innocent and guilty
Bodies sprawl
On the streets of Iraq

Kabul Palestine Israel
Who will be next
Syria Korea Iran

The world waits
Who will survive
The carnage

When the children ask
How it happens
Why

What shall we answer

Twelfth Summer

Walking from the lake, past the dark woods
I froze, hairs prickling on my arms, my nape,
hearing sharp treble screams like those
of a small child or infant, terror struck.

I pressed through tangled growth
toward the shrill sound and found
a tiny rabbit, struggling weakly,
impaled on a low branch.

I raced for help, relieved to see
the taciturn old man whose farm
stood closer than the summer boarding
house where family stayed.

He went into the barn and strode out
carrying a rifle, grousing. He had
work to do, no time for stupid,
careless animals, or kids.

He shot the rabbit twice, and breaking
off the branch, dangled the limp carcass,
swung it back and forth, the hot blood
splashing, and mocked, "Crybaby, you're
too big a girl to cry over a dumb rabbit."

"How old are you anyway? Eleven?
Twelve?" His bloody hand reached out and
slid snake-fast inside my bathing suit,
and squeezing hard, smeared each new breast.

Snickering, he flung the dripping,
still warm creature at my feet, poked at me
with his rifle and left me standing, paralyzed.
All these years later I still wonder:
How did he know that I would be afraid to tell?

In the hard dirt I buried the soft baby-thing.

BALLAD OF BLACK MAN WALKING

James Bird Jr., Jasper Texas, June 1998
"Here is a strange and bitter crop...."
—Strange Fruit

A man walking home
a hardworking man
walking alone
in soft summer twilight
lush scent of jasmine
filling the air.
A man looking forward
to dinner, to just sitting down
to rest in the shade.

A man who climbed quickly
into a truck
glad for a lift
easing the ache
of the last dusty miles.

When did he realize
when did he feel
the first clutch of terror?
Was it the high pitched
shrill of their laughter
the fumes of White Lightning
reek of white bodies
hot with excitement?

Hear the thud of his body
his cattle chained body
jerked over ruts, over stones

over miles of back country roads.
Hear his skull bursting open
face peeled in the grit
of dark southern soil.

And what of his kinfolk
his wife and his children?
Were they shown, did they see
those bright orange circles
marking places where parts
of his body were strewn?
Who gathered the shreds
the torn pulp of his body
to bring them in bags
with tatters of clothing
with shards of his scattered
broken sweet bones?

And how is it now
in the small town of Jasper?
Did they bury the anguish
the rage and the fear?
How much can be borne
how much be forgiven?

How much can be buried
along with the bones?

GOING THROUGH ARSENIC

I write to tell you you are not alone.

—Dylan Thomas

Poetry has saved me again and again.

—Muriel Rukeyser

GOING THROUGH ARSENIC
for Lucille

You say *Transplant*
A cold finger
traces my backbone
raises hair at my nape

You say don't worry
you are certain there's a match for you somewhere

I remind you that Ace used to remark
Out of all evil comes good, out of all good, evil.
Not like him to pontificate, but we agree that
life by God has taught us he was right

Which reminds you of an old miners' saying,
You have to go through arsenic to reach gold.

We speak then of that cruel transplant,
your ancestors torn from their homeland
chained as if less than cattle in fetid holds
of slaveships where only the strongest
could survive the journey
How those brutal voyages shaped, still shape
the lives of black and white these centuries later

Dear woman, strong Dahomey woman
you have endured enough to break Job's back
I must trust you will survive this passage
This time at last find healing gold

WEAVERS
for Lucille

Our friendship's blend
of black and white
rejects the needle's bite
the scissors blade

Through the long years
we've woven cloth
for binding wounds
dark robes for mourning
and from our
stubborn silver hair
wild skirts for dancing

AT ASILOMAR

Chrysanthemums

luminous

under noon sun

Remind me

suddenly

that hours ago

and miles

away

I left

a stovetop

gas ring

still alight

hot red-gold

petals flaming

MONARCH

We walked into the woods where Monarch
butterflies had clustered, covering branches
trunks of trees, their exotic wings
quivering, quivering, an amazement of color.

My friend clapped his large hands, filling the air
with a panic of orange flutter. For just a moment
I was crowned with a strange weight, a multitude
of delicate wings beating, clinging to my hair.

ESSENCE
OF BONNIE

Russet
Glowing

Ripe
Pomegranate

Within
Firm skin

Tender
Sweet
Surprises

NORA, CARE OF THE DOLLHOUSE
please forward

Dear Nora, when did you know
the air you breathed was dead
and that the dollhouse door
had grown too small
to squeeze through
carrying old luggage?

After you left it all behind
did you sometimes look back?
Tell me, was it hard
learning to start anew,
discovering at last
just who you really were?

I'm told that lately
you were seen out dancing,
not doing the tired
three steps forward
two steps back routine
but dancing cheek to cheek
with your new self, and Nora,
it was said that you were smiling.

SPRING DROUGHT
1978–1979, for Koala

Skyturtle stands
on the bank of the Eel

parched earth beneath his feet

The child and the woman
seek relief under his shadow

He sends up ancient prayers
through blinding sun motes

The river bed bends on itself
seeking what the sun drinks

The woman holds night
and its secrets in her hair

The child bathes in their flowing

MOON MAGIC   BIG SUR
for little John

Barefoot in his flannel robe
he pads cat-quiet from his room
stretches his skinny leg down
past the squeak-step   scarcely breathing
trembling in fear of being caught
fear of harsh voices, harsher hands
but drawn to the night moon's magic

He makes his way through shadowed woods
illumined by the full moon's swollen teat
to reach his secret ritual place;
unties the tasseled cord, lies naked
along the split trunk of a great fallen tree
sings in a thin clear treble
to his mother moon, asks that she send
her rays to enter him, to give him strength
then rising, closes his robe, his heart
Returns to the fear fraught house
where unlit hearts lie sleeping

OLD LIONESS

for Ellen Bass & baby Saraswati
1978

I watch you holding Sara
your two young faces
vulnerable in sleep
and keep this woman vigil,
seeing in you and in small Sara
what we must defend.

Once more I stretch
these war-scarred muscles
unsheath and sharpen
time-worn claws,
restrain this roar
of mother love
that swells,
alert for sound
or scent of danger.

I pace the darkness,
the open mouth of cave.

ON MEETING LAURIE'S NEW YOUNG SON
for Julie

A bantam monarch you survey the world
from a wheeled canvas throne. We delight in
your miniature perfection, touched
by your calm presumption of a safe domain.

Your mother hands you to her sister, where,
relaxed as unbaked dough, you drape yourself
against familiar density of warmth
and fall into complacent sleep.

Our talk turns to complexities you face,
skills you must acquire to survive this world.
A world we never would devise
if given a true voice in its conception.
And as we speak of dreams and seek solutions,
we surround you while we can, and shield you.

KOAN

I see the worm
burrow deep

It reappears

Severed it becomes
a pair of squirming parts

Hacked again
it simply multiplies

Refuses to disappear

What does the Bodhisattva
ask of this ignorant student?

MIXED WORKSHOP FLAMENCO

Castanets   sharp teeth
click counterpoint
to quick staccato beat
Arched backs circle
stilettos flash
are sheathed
Roses tossed
retrieved

OKLAHOMA CITY
April 19th, 1995

Her eyes search the room
the bunk beds
the door

Her voice, flat, repeats

Somebody should tell you
what to do
I don't know what to do

Do you leave
their things the way they are
their room like this

Do I give away their toys
their clothes
their beds

I don't know what to do

What do you say
when people ask
if you have children

Do you say no

Do you say I had two boys
two sons, two and four
They're dead

Somebody tell me
tell me
what to do

Brown Baby

"I want you to drink from the plenty cup"
        — lyric by Oscar Brown Jr.

On screen, skinny
wrists in handcuffs
a young mother,
arrested for leaving her baby
in a church vestibule.

I got three at home that's hungry,
I thought maybe this one
might have a chance.

REASSURANCE

Face, slab of old ham,
he hunkers on the curb
in weather that is kind.

Hearing shrill yelps
loud play cries of young boys,
his mind drifts to another time,

remembering stoop-ball,
ringelevio, kick-the-can,
remembering.

He thinks a pal has come
to roust him for a game of ball,
is poking at him with a bat.

Prodded, he wakes, confused.
Told to move on, he shuffles, aimless
searches his grainy pockets

for something, anything, cigar stub,
coin, a number scribbled on a scrap,
proof of existence.

EYE FOR AN EYE
9/11/2001

Unearthly explosion
hail of crushed concrete
clouds of ash and debris
stampede of humans
fleeing in panic
a grandson of mine
running blindly
among them

When at last he could see
the girl who was clinging
to his hand as they ran
he saw in her eyes
a look of pure terror
never encountered
still not forgotten

A friend told him after
of standing transfixed
of watching in horror
as people rained down
from a surreal sky
The thud of their impact
sound of their bursting
repeating repeating
at night in his dreams

And what can we say
or do for the living
but pray they have strength
ask for their healing

Blessed be the mourners
whose lives have been shattered
all those lives that were shattered
through no fault of their own

Blessed be the peacemakers
who see through the curtains
of greed and of lies
who are willing to risk
to bring peace to our lives
and refuse to obey
the cruel senseless credo
An eye for an eye

TRANSGRESSOR

He wears
the narrowed
eyes
tight lips
taut chin
of one
whose credo
is weaponry

He turns
huge keys
reckless
of what will
be unlocked

He labels
masses of
innocents
mutilated
and mangled
or mercifully dead
Collateral Damage

He mouths
Freedom
Democracy
as they are
furtively
eroded

He imposes
his will
blind to
the future

the bloodbath
his children
our children
all children
may drown in

YERBA MATÉ

Laughter is the most surefire healant I know.

—Toni Cade Bambara

ON MY OWN

Lonely old men
follow me
in the supermarket
think I look like
a good cook
well padded
white haired
safe.
Say things like
"Scuse me, Can you tell me
how long do I boil eggplant?" or
"Are these greens okay to microwave?"

Sometimes
my heart wants
to take them home
set their frail
stooped shoulders
soft little paunches
skinny tired legs
right down in the kitchen.
Let them watch
as I stir the gravy
sift and slice

fetch out the leftover pie
add the ice cream,
ask, "Would you like me to
iron that shirt for you
wouldn't take but a minute"
see their rheumy eyes light up.

If I knew they'd go right on home
never darken my door again
I might even do that.
But, let's be honest, there's no pie
in my old fridge; even the ironing
board has forgotten the stroke of my hand.

EXAMINING THE MYTH
Dorset, Vermont

Observe
a veritable
paint by number
stone-fenced
white-steepled
red-barned view.
Fat dollops
of creamy clouds
float o'er green fields
against a sky
of blatant
azure blue.
Behold the herd
of sturdy cows
all neatly black on white.
See here and there
a pumpkin patch
a skein of geese in flight.
Now add a flock
of fleecy lambs
then dare to tell us who
it was that claimed that these
restrained
New Englanders
would never ever overdo.

AFTER THE BALL WAS....

It was that time, a little more than halfway
through the party. Too many Margaritas
and the heat of Samba steamed the air as
couples danced, no longer with their mates.

The hot white moon rippled an invitation
across the pool's cool face, and they
screamed with laughter as the town clown
took a running dive and leaped right in.

Next thing you know the whole damn gang was hooting
and hollering, tossing their clothes all mixed up together
onto the pool's edge, and all those middle-aged bodies
mixed up together in the water. Lord, it was something
else.

Next morning there wasn't hardly a thing to show the
wild time had by all. Nothing but a limp corn plaster
settled at the bottom of the pool, some happy faces,
oh, and a few worried frowns around town.

THEY DANCE BOVINELY

apologies to John Lennon & A Spaniard In the Works

here comes the ride
in a vale
of illusion
the gloom
dazing into
her contracts
hears
an indifferent drummer
the music
is lower grins
bedding starch
as they false
dapperly
error after

truck stop
found poem

hey momma
jay walkin'
in that tight
red dress
your ass
just don't turn green
you're holdin' up traffic

YERBA MATÉ AT P.S.73
1930

We hang our coats in the wardrobe
it smells stale and musty
The lavatory smells like Pine-sol and pee
the big girls giggle and whisper
at the mirror

I hate school

Every morning my stomach aches
my father says I am being difficult

Classes are dumb
I draw pictures and pass notes
from Chester to Lillian

Lillian is blonde and skinny
she can climb the rope in gym

I hate gym

There's a big fence
around the schoolyard
Every day at recess there's
this dumb dog who runs
back and forth barking

I throw him half my sandwich
and pretend he's waiting for me

I call him Chester

It seems like Mr. Crowe is scared
of the big boys
He bangs on his desk with
his ring and yells "Order! Order!"
They don't pay any attention

It gives me a headache

I think Mr. Crowe has eyes
for Miss Rooney. She has red hair
and big you know whats
Her desk is open in front
The big boys try to sit in the front row
they grin and poke each other

She pretends not to notice

Miss Crowley teaches geography. I hate geography
but I love Miss Crowley. Her voice is soft
and she smiles at me. I learn about South America
They drink a weird tea called Yerba Maté

Sometimes I dream

I dream about sitting under a palm tree
with Miss Crowley. She pours strange liquid
into a cup and says, "Have some Yerba Maté."

I drink it, and Zappo! I am transformed.

WHEN I WAS LITTLE

I got a new baby brother.
He has funny lumpy
things in front.
The one in the middle
sticked out sometimes.
My mother told me
it was his peepee. Poor baby.

I asked her if the doctor
could take it off, like he
took off the wart on my finger.
She said the baby needed it
for number one. I wished
he could have a nice smooth
secret place, like mine.

One day in the vestibule
an old man opened his overcoat
and showed me his. *Yccch!*
And once, when I was going to
music lesson on the bus
a man held up the newspaper
on his lap and said I could
peek at a surprise

It must have bothered him a lot.
He was trying to pull it off.
Stuff like that made me worry
a whole lot for my little brother.

So I told my father and mother and
my father laughed real hard and said
I had a bad case of some kind of envy.
He stopped laughing when he saw
my mom had her pruned up face on.
I guess she was worrying too.

SURE CURE

Yes
there are other men
she finds attractive
Who stimulate
present intriguing
questions in her mind
And she admits
that she is prone
to fantasize
But then
she pictures them
with soft boiled
yawning morning faces
and all illicit
thought of romance dies

POLITICS VS. CHICKEN LITTLE

Oh yes my little darlings
my dearies, my precious ones
Oh yes the sky is falling
the sky is falling down
She squawks it up and down the street
my dearies, my little ones
She cackles through the marketplace
and all around the town
But no one wants to hear it
to hear it is to fear it
So everyone is silent
and deaf in our good town

LOOKING BACK

I. High School Prom

Queen of the prom
a carrot dangles
from her scepter
Favors bestowed
withdrawn
Beauty and talent
with a certain flair
for decimating
competition
Most Likely to Succeed
Most Popular
the yearbook reads
Neglecting to include
most feared

II. High School Reunion

Her fourth martini
this one sipped
Her eyes dart over men
like flies on picnic fare
Three husbands
combat stripes
dumped in a drawer
with other war mementos
She shrugs   leans toward me
still with studied
elegance of line   to hiss
"The same man after all these
years. God what a bore!"
and flicks her ashes
on my life once more

UFO

Yr poetry
Is too literal
He said

Just wing it

Try to write
Off the top
Of yr head

Now it's up
There

Somewhere

AT A CONFERENCE FOR WOMEN

Many years ago
the guest speaker, prim
in suburban matron drag,
blue-white coiffure,
knit suit and Gucci bag,
stepped to the podium.
Typecast, the perfect
corporation wife, who
with her opening sentence
changed my life.

I once had forty tits
and someone dragging
on each one.
I now have two,
they both belong to me,
and life is much more fun.

The rest of her remarks
remain a blur,
but I am down to three.
Blue-haired deceptive lady,
I'm almost running free.

WHISTLE STOP

The old storyteller has been on every journey.
It is the task of the storyteller to pass on the truth,
so that nothing is forgotten....

—Leslie Marmon Silko

Four Seasons In Apricot

I thought some of you might be curious about what goes on at a writing workshop, so I'd like to share a recent experience with you. A friend brought me a jar of apricots. Sun poured through the jar on the window sill, and I was inspired to write the following poem, which I took to the workshop to be critiqued. Well, it was.

> Apricot blossoms
> Fragile dancers
> Sway
> in sunlight
>
> Apricots ripen
> Plump monks
> Sunning
> in saffron robes
>
> Apricots captured
> Sun planets
> Golden globes
> in jars
>
> Apricot liqueur
> Glides down
> Molten sun
> inside

Lisa felt the first stanza had been said before. She was right.

I just couldn't think of a better way to say it. So,
I scratched stanza one.

Claire, who has an apricot orchard and cans the fruit,
rather liked the description in stanza three. No one
else did, so I bequeathed it to her, with love. May her
shelves be filled with gleaming, glowing, golden
globes (we had just discussed alliteration).

No one could agree whether the molten sun of the
liqueur should glide down and become molten sun
inside, or just glide down. So, I bought a pint of
apricot brandy on the way home. Next morning I
couldn't remember what decision I had come to, and
added a footnote saying lines two and three of stanza
four may be inverted at the reader's discretion. But
that seemed lacking in self-determination.

So, stanzas 3 and 4 and 1 ... aced out.

Susan felt the whole poem was overly tidy. She was
right. I just hoped no one would notice. However,
everyone agreed that stanza 2, the one with the
plump monks sunning in saffron robes, was a quite
picturesque turn of phrase.

This morning, there it stood, all by itself, looking
lonely, but somehow—I thought—rather Zenny.

WHISTLE STOP

Mornin' sir, jest thought I'd stop by and say welcome. We're sure glad you decided to settle hereabouts and open the old Feed 'n Grain again. This store's sure been missed since old Luther went to his reward. Farmers hereabouts been takin turns goin inta Harveyville loadin a truck or two, but it sure weren't no convenience.

Jest come from havin a cup a coffee at the Station. Well, it's a restaurant now. Not one a your big fancy ones. Jest the old whistle stop depot in Hewlett. By the way, that's HewLETT, notice you're sayin HEWlett the way them tourists do. Anyways, you oughta come by an try some a Alma's cookin. Not too bad, an it's a good place to meet folks, you bein a stranger an all.

There's old pictures of railroads an railroad men on the walls, cept behind the counter where there's a rack a name mugs. Must be close to forty of em, Art, Wally, Everett, Ralph...known most all of em since they was tads. After chores are done lot of em like to stop by for a cup an jaw about what's goin on. Gotta change outta your muck boots though, else

Alma, she's the owner, makes you set out on the steps.
Suits fine most the year, but you could freeze your
tiddlywinks off come winter.

We're startin to get tourists stoppin in lately.
Jest now, jest afore I left the Depot, one a them tourists
complains he's found a slice a tater stuck under his
hotcakes, 'n sides that his eggs was tough. Alma, she's
the owner, says loud enough for all to hear, "Say, you
tell im that's the way we like things round here. Tough.
N'bout that tater, no charge."

Snickers all around, folks sneakin a look. Well,
the fella gets up, throws a couple of dollar bills on the
table an walks out. Can't say I blame him. Anyways,
Purleen, that's the waitress, skinny as a bird what got
pushed out the nest too soon, stands jest lookin out
after him like she lost somethin. Well, he was different
than what she's used to lookin at, that's for sure.
Wouldna done her no good anyhow. So shy she cain't
hardly ask do you want cream for your coffee. Funny.
She's got a one track mind. Has to finish with one
table afore she can start up another. Folks round here
used to waitin. No place else much to go anyhows.
Sides, she's Ed Talbert's young'n. Both her folks gone.

Lost her pa in a railroad accident, her ma to sugar diabetes an her only brother a name on that there wall down to Washington.

They was good people, an truth to tell, Purleen, she never were too bright. Got a sister some older was livin to Abilene. Ran off with some guy what come to the county seat for the fair. Don't nobody hear from her. Not for a long spell. So, guess we all kinda look after Purleen.

Well, gotta mosey. Glad you come to town. Like I said, folks here missed the store after old Luther died, so, you're already welcome. Jest give it a chance, reckon you'll find HewLETT's not a bad place to be.

THE LOCK

I love my daddy to read to me. He mostly reads stuff I don't understand. The words are real long but in the story I can guess what they probably mean. I like to sit on his lap and lean against him. His voice is real deep and if I press my ear against his vest I get shivers through it from his voice. It tickles my ear.

He likes to read to me but he never reads my books or the funny papers. In fact he likes sad stuff a lot. Long poems like *The Wreck of the Hespress*, where a little girl and her father drown in a boat in a big storm even though he tied her to the mast, or *Evangeline* where this girl and her boyfriend are trying to find one another but they pass right by each other without knowing, and they never, never met. Oh and he likes scary poems too. Once he showed me the house where the man who wrote that creepy one about the raven lived, but he's dead now. His name was Edgar, just like my father, except he had a funny last name, I think it was Po.

Last Sunday when Aunt Carrie came Daddy showed me a envelope she gave him. It had paper in it like you get inside birthday presents. You know, the crinkly, whispery kind; and he opened it and showed me a pressed flat curl of white hair with a little black ribbon bow on it. He said it was Grandma's hair from when she died and Aunt Carrie cut off a piece for all the uncles and aunts in their family.

He had such a sad face, but he kept looking at me like I wasn't being sad enough too. Which I wasn't cause she was real strict and I liked Grandma Barrett a whole lot better which I didn't tell him, ever. Then he started to tell me how bad I would feel when *my* mommy died and all I had was a piece of her hair, only he called it a lock. It made me so sad I started to cry. And he took out his hanky and wiped my face and said I was his good little girl. Then I felt better because he didn't look sad anymore.

A Tired Long Way From Little Rock

This mornin I knocked on Miz Whitman's door and called, "Ag, you ready?" She didn answer so I figgered she musta gone down a mite early, cause last night the aide reminded us this here's the mornin we get muffins steada plain toast. An I'm here to tell you that if you're late, they're gone. Either they don't never make enough, or some folks is "Mr. Greedy" an grabs extra to sneak up to their room.

You know how they are bout havin food in your room. They took Ag's plant away, they're that fussy. Said the damp soil would draw bugs quick as crumbs. Landsakes, I had plants indoors all my grown life an they didn never draw bugs. Truth to tell, them aides probly didn want to be bothered waterin it. Aggie cried like a baby. It was from her son in Texarkana, the one she sets such store by.

But that daughter, Ginny, the one Ag give up her farm an come out here to be close-by to! She's all the time fussin at Ag fer bein so forgetful, or fer gettin stains onto her frontage. Forever fiddlin, tuggin at Aggie's skirts, pullin em down past her knees. Tellin her she shoulda wore a short sleeve dress cause it's warm, else a sweater cause it might get cold. When she goes over Ag's bill, she takes on fer ever little extra nickel. Has a spasm if a long distance call shows up. She don't understand there's times Ag gets so she just has to talk to her boy, an he don't call too often.

She stops by regular as cow's milk an takes Ag to meetin ever Sunday. Plops her down in the pew like a sack a meal what's got weevils, an off she goes to visit till time for service. Folks always sayin how nice to see sech a lovin daughter holdin her ma's hand all through sermon. Truth is that's jest so she can squeeze real hard an wake Ag up when she starts to nod! Aggie don't hardly hear nor see that good, so she don't much enjoy goin to church. It's the gettin out. A ride an a whiff a fresh air.

She don't care fer the air conditionin here. Says it makes her dizzy, and the noise keeps her awake. Says if they didn keep the windows sealed we'd all be heavin ourselves out! She's a card that one, feisty too. Told me that on her birthday when she got took to her daughter's fer family dinner she got tired a them all talkin past her like she weren't there. Sayin things like "Mebbe she's sleepy," or "Think we best get her to the bathroom fore we take her back?" Said she finally spoke up. "I ain't two year old, an I got my hearin aid *on* and my teeth *in,* so jest speak up an I'll be pleased to answer fer myself!"

But there I go, natterin on, an I was tellin you bout Aggie not bein in her room when I stopped by. She weren't down to breakfast neither, an when I come

124

back past, her door was wide open. I tell you, it hurt to see. That daughter a hers was throwin things inta one a them Goodwill bags quick as you please, an a course I knowed Ag musta gone in the night.

I felt real bad, cause Ag was that scared a dyin alone. Anyone coulda tole she was failin. I give her that Bang Alarm my grandniece sent me fer Christmas. Told her to keep it handy on her night stand. I said, "You jest bang on that thing an the whole staff'll be in here afore you can make yourself decent." But you know Agnes, "Never complain, never explain," that was her motto. An she never. Leastways not that I ever heard. But she was a real worrier, always frettin an worryin.

Anyways, I didn stop to ask no particulars. Bad news travels fast enough an I'm in no hurry. Lord knows I'm not goin nowhere. Jest shows, makes no sense worryin. All the same, wish I'd a thought to ask for my Bang Alarm.

MS. MALAPROP SPEAKS

My dad asked me why I broke up with my financee.
When I asked did he want the details he said,
Absolutely, just run it up the old scrotum pole.

Well, as of last month
I illuminated Herbie from my life. He is now completely
persona au gratin.

At first he fulfilled all my exploitations, and for
all intensive purposes I thought we had reached a real
platitude of understanding, and life with him would be
a venerable Paradise.

We even had our furniture picked out, French Prevential.

Everyone thought he was such an extinguished man.
He had very epileptic taste, and always dressed in
designered clothes, you know, like Melvin Klein.
He was very self-insured, and I thought that I was lucky
to hook up with such an affluential family, but after
a while I saw that they were real religious phonetics.
Sure they were always talking botherly love,
but just the same, telling anti-semantic antidotes
and mocking anybody different from them.

Things got worse, when he told me his mother said that
I was the necrotic type who would probably suffer from
UPS and that while she believed in consensible sex
between consulting adults, to her mind only a cramp
would live with someone before they were married.

Well, I really resembled that, and said she was trying to
break us up. Then he said I took her words out of
contest and then I said he had an Edifice contest
and well, every thing just escalatored. The things he said
were so mean, they're inedibly printed on my mind.
Oh, I could've died.

Well, my father said Herbert had a really poor altitude.
I guess he's right; Herbie got only three votes when
he ran for Town Council at the last erection.

So my father gave me his charge card and
said if I was like my mother, shopping was the best
anecdote for heartbreak.
I can't wait to show you my new outfits.

OF BEARDS, BOWLS & BATONS

King Arthur was there, and his beard was white and beautiful. It gleamed with a strange light. The three kings were there too, with beautiful gifts of gold and rubies, and sapphires the size of eggs! And King Wenceslas was there and Merlin and Sophocles, all their white beards shining with wisdom. Oh, they were splendid, they all were holding strange pink and purple batons, and when they spoke, all their batons rose right up and waved proudly in the air.

Then they spoke in big deep voices, all at the same time, "We Command You with our wonderful batons." And just then, Mary appeared. She was up on the ceiling, just like the one Michael Angelo painted. Oh, he was there too, but his beard was dripping with paint. It looked yucky! Of course Mary was dressed in blue, that deep blue I loved before they went and cleaned the ceiling and all the angels and saints showed up in dumb candy colors.

I wanted to ask Mr. Angelo how he felt about that, but just then Mary leaned down and held out this big bowl, and she said, "Here, take and eat of this, and you will enter the Kingdom, and be saved." So I asked, "Saved for what?" Then Mary looked kind of crabby like Sister Anna Teresa, when you ask a dumb question in class, so I looked in the bowl, and it was full of worms!

Well! I got kind of mad and I said, "Oh! I've eaten all the worms I need to, and I've obeyed all the batons I had to. So, I don't think I want to enter the kingdom right now. But thank you anyway, for the invitation."

And then, with one big boomy voice the Kings asked, "Are you afraid?" So I answered, "Well, wait just a minute— what kingdom are we talking about? Because I just want to know before I do any entering." But they wouldn't answer, and they all turned their backs on me– and all their batons just drooped!

All of a sudden I felt light as air, and I rose up higher and higher. Higher than their boomy voices or their dumb batons could reach, and right past Mary, who wouldn't even look at me!

And then, there they were, all of them around me. No, not the Kings. All my deary loved ones, that I've been missing and longing to see. But there were so many all at once and their arms were reaching for me, and their hands, and their voices became a great babble– and I WOKE UP!!! And I thought, "Self, you better write this one down, and pense on it."

Standing Invitation

It was irritating
waking up, then falling back into the same tedious dream.
Ordinary people seated around an ordinary table
in an ordinary house. Faces vaguely familiar, ho-hum
conversation. More people arriving, seating themselves,
exchanging banal greetings.

All at once
everything changes, no rhyme or reason. I stand
at the top of several incredibly long, almost blindingly
white flights of stairs. So steep I have vertigo...dizzy,
nauseous. Yet I can't stop myself
from looking down.

A voice
from somewhere behind me says, "Of course it seems
different, we added another floor and a roof."
Well that's it. That's all I remember.

Anyway
quite often since then—that was a week or so ago—
I find myself daydreaming, anywhere, anytime, day or
night, staring down that angular, steep stairwell, leaning
toward that black pinhole at the very bottom.

Then suddenly
I snap out of it, breathing fast, my heart doing a reggae,
a sensation I haven't had since the bad old days when I
went back and forth to work in the city.

You'll think
this is wacko, but back then I had this compulsion, this
urge, standing as close as possible to the very, very edge
of the platform above the subway tracks, holding my
breath, feeling the vibration through the soles
of my feet, my whole body, as the train approached
my body taut, waiting.

Waiting
for that *rush*. For the train to come roaring, barreling out
of that deep black tunnel. Each time drawn forward,
feeling that pull, that urgency, each time,
wondering.

HONDURAS

I am expecting a friend; we are going
shopping. While waiting I pick up Solidarity, a
magazine I have been meaning, but not making time,
to peruse.

On the cover is an arresting photo of a young
woman whose guarded eyes evade mine. I turn the
page, learn that her name is Lesly Rodriguez. Lesly is
fourteen; she will rise at four a.m., dress, wait for the
yellow school bus to pick her up. She dreams a big
dream for a woman child in Honduras. Of learning a
skill, of going to school, a decent wage, decent life.

She takes her seat in the bus with other girls.
None are younger than eleven, none older than
sixteen. The bus does not take them to school, but to
a fenced-in factory where they are herded into a
cavernous room crowded with plank tables, boxes
filled with skeins of wool and young girls, six
hundred of them.

The workplace is not alive with the chatter
and easy laughter of young girls. That is forbidden.
What they hear are the foremen's voices urging,
rapido, rapido, ten, twelve hours a day. Supervisors
who touch them as they search for hidden sweets
which might stain the fabric they work on for
Norteamericano designers and manufacturers whose
familiar names command high prices. These girls

work for one hundred and eighty-eight lempiras, about twenty-one dollars, per week. No extra for overtime. Our government is aware of this.

I would prefer to write a new poem, a funny story, a love sonnet, than what seems to many like the same old propaganda. New trade laws, and the politics of silence abetting secrecy, force me to speak my anger, to act on it, when I learn that I, like you, am wearing, as we all in our blind ignorance or indifference wear, the sweat of helpless children on our backs.

MARIA SEZ

for my dear friend Rosa Maria

Hey, I gotta talk to you. You know I think I'm goin outta my friggin mind an I gotta talk to you. What I wanna know is how do you live through it...all the shit. You've lived through it an I gotta know how. Every night I go to bed an my mind goes crazy...I start hittin the bottle an I can't sleep. I gotta sleep...I'm goin to school an takin care of five kids.

Ramon, he's the thirteen year old, you know, he's gettin into trouble. Shit, drugs, you know, bad company. Hey, the twelve year old, he's followin right behind him!

The girls, they don give me no trouble, an the baby. I tell them, "Look at the baby, she's two years old, so what do I have to teach her, to walk, to talk, to shit in the pot. I awreddy taught you that, so why do you hang on my tit? You gotta let go!"

Hey...the other night I went nuts...Ramon stands there friggin smart ass an he sez, "I don gotta do no dishes." An I said, "Wotta you mean you don gotta do no dishes...do I ask you to support me, to feed me, to wash my clothes, my ass? All I'm askin is for you to do the dishes so I can study." An he just stands there smart ass an sez, "I don gotta do them, thass for women." An I went crazy, I picked up a stick I keep in the house—you know, there's always

134

weirdos hangin aroun this block—an I hit him over the head with it an I split his scalp, an I grab hol of his hair an the blood is runnin through my fingers an down his face an I'm sayin, "Mothafuckah, I gave you life! I gave you life an I can give you death just as easy. Easier!

"I can go to jail an they can cook my meals an do my laundry. I can sit on my ass at night an write poems an I can make it with the dykes an not have to bother with no lousy men fuckin over me! You think I can't kill you? It's an easy out for me. You do what I say or take your ass down to L.A. Go fine your father. Let him worry about you."

Hey, you know I love this kid, an I come close to killin him. An I gotta talk to you. How you lived through all your shit. How you still live through it.

FIRST MYSTERY

Was I five, six, seven? No way to remember exactly.
Leaning on the window sill on a humid stifling day,
too hot to go outdoors, I saw a group of several naked
young boys diving from a makeshift dock into the Harlem
River. They were too far to clearly hear or see, but I
watched with envy their carefree leap and splash. Then, as
if in slow motion, the boys climbed from the water and
gathered, staring down into the murk.

Within minutes grownups appeared, and then police.
Stunned, I watched as a small body was lifted from the
water, laid motionless on the planks, and covered.

For the first time death, it's abrupt irrevocable finality, held
real meaning. And for the first of countless times
I questioned how one could be laughing, playing, as that
boy was, so joyously, buoyantly alive, yet in an instant
become only a silent shell, suddenly, absolutely still.

And at eighty-three I still question, is there instant peace,
that blessed nothingness that death implies, or will an
amazing adventure await?

In either case, I am ready.

COLOPHON

Adobe's Robert Slimbach designed this postscript text type *Minion* in 1989. Its shape is based on hot type created by Nicolas Jenson in Mainz in 1470, Venetian printer & publisher Aldus Manutius and his punch-cutter, Francesco Griffo in 1501, and the Parisian Claude Garamond in 1545. The roman typeface continues to conform to new print technology, especially with the 1967 *Sabon* designed by Jan Tschichold. *Minion* has a legible and pleasant appeal, and is well suited for printing poetry because of its clean feet, well proportioned small caps and text figures.

MANY NAMES PRESS
KATE HITT
POST OFFICE BOX 1038
CAPITOLA, CALIFORNIA USA
95010-1038

Currently available through Small Press Distribution,
www.maudemeehan.com, www.manynamespress.com
& locally-owned, independent bookstores everywhere